Routes of
Cross-Cultural
Exchange

Trade Routes to India

Bridey Heing

Cavendish Square
New York

Published in 2018 by Cavendish Square Publishing, LLC
243 5th Avenue, Suite 136, New York, NY 10016

First Edition

Cataloging-in-Publication Data

Names: Heing, Bridey.
Title: Trade routes to India / Bridey Heing.
Description: New York : Cavendish Square, 2018. | Series: Routes of cross-cultural exchange | Includes index.
Identifiers: ISBN 9781502626943 (library bound) | ISBN 9781502626882 (ebook)
Subjects: LCSH: Trade routes--India--History--Juvenile literature. | India--Commerce--History--Juvenile literature. | Asia--Commerce--Europe--Juvenile literature. | Europe--Commerce--Asia--Juvenile literature.
Classification: LCC HF3785.H45 2018 | DDC 388'.0440954--dc23

Editorial Director: David McNamara
Editor: Caitlyn Miller
Copy Editor: Alex Tessman
Associate Art Director: Amy Greenan
Designer: Jessica Nevins
Production Coordinator: Karol Szymczuk
Photo Research: J8 Media

The photographs in this book are used by permission and through the courtesy of: Cover Maritiem Museum Rotterdam/Wikimedia Commons/File:Jacob van Strij - Het jacht van de kamer Rotterdam begroet eenOostindiëvaarder.jpg/CCO; p. 5 Pool Benainous/Tinacci/Gamma-Rapho/Getty Images; p. 8 Smith Collection/Gado/Archive Photos/Getty Images; p. 10 Dinodia Photo/Passage/Getty Images; p. 11 ©iStock.com/ZU_09; p. 16 Wrangel/iStock/Thinkstock; p. 18 Universal History Archive/ Universal Images Group/Getty Images; p. 20 DEA/G. Nimatallah/De Agostini/Getty Images; p. 23 PHGCOM/Wikimedia Commons/File:ChandraguptaIIOnHorse.jpg/CC BY-SA 3.0; p. 30 Asanka Brendon Ratnayake/Lonely Planet Images/Getty Images; p. 32 FreeShot/iStock/Thinkstock; p. 35 Annie Owen/robertharding/Getty Images; p. 40 mdsharma/Shutterstock.com; p. 45 DEA Picture Library/De Agostini Picture Library/Getty Images; p. 47 ©iStock.com/duncan1890; p. 51 zhaojiankang/iStock/Thinkstock; p. 53 adoc-photos/Corbis Historical/Getty Images; p. 56 Tethys Imaging LLC/Shutterstock.com; pp. 62, 66 saiko3p/iStock/Thinkstock; p. 72 monotoomono/ Shutterstock.com; p. 80 Noah Seelam/AFP/Getty Images; p. 81 Frederic Legrand – COMEO/ Shutterstock.com; p. 82 WPA Pool/Getty Images; p. 84 Srikar Kashyap/Wikimedia Commons/ File:Garikapati Narasimha Rao in March 2015.JPG/CC BY-SA 4.0.

Printed in the United States of America

Table of Contents

Introduction

India, a Connection Between East and West

For much of its history, India has been at the heart of trade between the Eastern and Western worlds. Located in Southeast Asia on the border between the Middle East and China with access to the South Pacific and Africa via the Indian Ocean, India has a rich history of connecting people and places through trade. Goods made in India, such as spices and art objects, were influential around the world. The country served as an important stop on the Silk Road and other major trade routes on land. In the country's role as meeting place between the East and West, India was the heart of cross-cultural communication between the world's empires for centuries.

India's importance to trade dates back to the ancient world, when trade routes were just developing. Sea routes connecting Africa to the

The Silk Road, shown here on a piece of fabric, connected East and West by both land and sea.

empires of the Mediterranean were established, while land routes connected China to the Middle East. These routes allowed for the sharing of food, goods, religion, artistic styles, and culture. And these exchanges shaped the development of the world as we know it.

Trade was an important part of the economy for India's first known civilization. The **Indus Valley Civilization** emerged around 3300 BCE. For two thousand years, it grew into one of the ancient world's strongest centers. Trade was the cornerstone of the Indus Valley's economy, with trade evolving along several lines. Religious pilgrimages between major towns in the area eventually developed into trade routes. As civilizations began establishing relations with one another through trade, India became a major center for commerce.

For centuries, Indian merchants and traders carried goods, foods, and culture with them across empires and civilizations. They connected the continents of the Southern Hemisphere, serving as a stopping point between Africa and China. They facilitated some of the most important trade routes in human history, including the Silk Road and the **Spice Trade**. India was key in establishing the foundation for the modern economy, pushing navigation, exploration, and economic growth forward for cultures around the world.

Indian trade routes included both land and sea routes, connecting Indian merchants and traders to the entire ancient world. The oldest road in Asia was established in India around the third century BCE, called the **Grand Trunk Road**. It linked the eastern and western boundaries of India, beginning in modern-day Bangladesh in the east and ending in modern-day Kabul, Afghanistan. At around 1,600 miles (2,574.9 kilometers), it was also the longest road in the ancient world. It served to connect the entire expansive **subcontinent** and served as a connection between East and West.

Other routes soon followed. The **Incense Route** of the third and second centuries CE ran through India, as did the legendary Silk Road of the first century CE. Around the time of the Silk Road, sea routes became key to Roman trade, and India played a large role in trade with the Mediterranean, Africa, and China. During the seventh and eighth centuries CE, the Spice Route further solidified India's role as a key power in international trade. Until the sixteenth century CE,

India was one of the wealthiest civilizations in the world.

But that changed in the later years of the **Maratha Empire**, when a famine killed a large percentage of the population and the economy began to suffer. In 1765, The **British East India Company** was established in Bengal, diverting profits from India to Great Britain. British colonial rule expanded into the twentieth century. The colonial administration took control of key Indian **exports**, stifling India's long-standing trade relations with the rest of the world. The legacy of colonialism impacted India's trade for decades after independence. Yet today, foreign trade has strengthened the country's economy, serving as yet another chapter in the ongoing story of Indian trade.

India has a long and rich history of trade that reflects the changing world in which the country grew. From the days of empires to the modern era, India has been at the forefront of trade and cross-cultural exchange. In this book, we will explore how trade routes developed both on land and sea, the goods that were traded between India and other civilizations, the way culture was exchanged via these trade routes, and how India's trade impacted history.

Chapter 1

Trade Before Indian Trade Routes

India has played an important role in global trade from the earliest days of human history. The ancient world had elaborate and complex trade routes. Many of these trade networks passed through India to connect the Mediterranean civilizations with the **Far East**. Sea routes also stopped in India en route to Africa and the South Pacific. Along with the modern Middle East, India made up the heart of the ancient world's great civilizations. The culture of India greatly influenced the goods being traded around the world.

Trade in the ancient world was slow and difficult. Dangers ranged from shipwrecks to robbery while on the routes that connected the world. But our understanding of trade in the ancient world is limited, making it difficult to establish strict

Opposite: *Salt and spices have played an important role in Indian trade for centuries.*

India was a center of culture in the ancient world, where epics like the Ramayana and Mahabharata were written. Both epics are shown in this series of murals on the ceiling of Chennakeshavaraya Temple.

dates when trade relations were established or trade routes were created. We rely on artifacts discovered and some formal records kept by rulers, including those of the Egyptians and Greeks. Dating goods found in one part of the world that were believed to be created in another helps historians estimate timelines. This process tells us when trade was taking place and what kinds of goods were being exchanged.

In the case of India, things become more difficult because India was a hub of trade for so much of human history. The Spice Routes, which lasted for many centuries, are believed to have been established around 3000 BCE. This was fifteen hundred years before the **Phoenicians** grew into the leading traders of their time and almost two thousand years before the Silk Road was established in the Far East. In short, the history of Indian trade is the history of trade for humankind.

Ships, like this galley built by the Phoenicians, were among the ancient world's most important trade advances.

The Influence of Nomads

There was a time before widespread trade in the ancient world. Thousands of years ago, mankind was mostly nomadic. People moved with the seasons and followed herds of animals they hunted. That began to change in the Paleolithic and Neolithic periods as formerly nomadic people began settling down to live in villages. This gave rise to specialization, or the development of certain skills that allowed people to take up trades. Originally, these communities were **self-sufficient**, producing what they needed to survive. But that changed as villages came into contact with one another through the very same routes they had used when they were nomads. Trade started to grow as farmers or artisans sought to exchange their excess goods for things they couldn't make or grow themselves.

One of the first goods traded widely was **obsidian**. Evidence has been found that the volcanic stone was traded as early as the Stone Age. Experts also think it was traded in Guinea as early as 17,000 BCE. By 12,000 BCE obsidian was being traded in the Mediterranean, along with other goods between Anatolia (or modern Turkey), the Middle East, and Egypt. In China, trade remained regional, and smaller kingdoms within China traded with one another. This changed as Chinese rulers consolidated power and sought to build relationships with other civilizations. Control of trade would allow empires to flourish and expand for centuries, and trade routes became the central source of income and exchange.

Changing Relationships

Trade relations started with nearby civilizations, such as the Phoenician city of Byblos in the **Levant** with Egypt between 4000 and 3000 BCE. Trade that covered much larger areas, such as trade between Greece and India or China and the Levant, required special technology. The domestication of camels in **Arabia** made it possible to travel over the dry lands between the Far East and the Mediterranean. Ships were also developed that could safely carry precious cargo overseas. The Phoenicians' ability to develop ships that sat high in the water and were weighted in the back made it possible for them to travel safely through the choppy waters of the Mediterranean. This innovation revolutionized their trade network. Over time, trade grew to include luxury goods, foods, art, and cultural exchange.

Although it took centuries, trade networks in the ancient world eventually connected the major civilizations in Europe, Asia, Arabia, and Africa. Routes went as far north as Great Britain, where traders sourced tin, and as far south the mid-African coast. Trade networks allowed empires from the Greeks to the Chinese to the Indians to influence their world and amass large fortunes that fed their expansion and fueled the ancient world.

In India, trade led to the growth of cities and allowed India to become one of the strongest global economies. But before trade became common, India was made up of small and isolated villages that produced their own food and goods. Mohenjo-daro

The Land of Punt

The Land of Punt was an ancient kingdom that traded frequently with Egypt. Although there is debate about where Punt was geographically, many believe it was on the **Horn of Africa** in modern-day Somalia. It might have been centered around Somalia's Puntland province. The kingdom traded in many goods, including trees, ebony, leopard skins, spices, and animals. What we know about Punt comes from Egyptian writings and inscriptions, particularly those made during the reign of Queen Hatshepsut. Hatshepsut traveled to Punt herself in 1493 BCE, a journey that at that time would have been incredibly long and dangerous. Although Hatshepsut oversaw one of the most prosperous times in Egyptian history, inscriptions suggest that her expedition to Punt was something she considered a great accomplishment.

Trade between Punt and Egypt was significant for many reasons. There is evidence that Egypt began trading with Punt as early as 2613 BCE, around the time when India's trade cities were flourishing. Trees brought from Punt to Egypt were used for the first known transplant of plant life.

Punt became an important part of Egypt's culture. Writings suggest that many Egyptians saw Punt as their place of origin, and the Egyptians called the kingdom the "Land of the Gods." Although little is known about the kingdom itself, today Punt is considered one of the forerunners of the great trading cultures of the ancient world, and an important part of the trading ecosystem that allowed Egypt and others to flourish.

and Harappa were the first major cities in what would become the Indus Valley civilization. Both were major trading capitals of the ancient world. They were established around 3000 BCE and grew into urban centers. Similarly, Kerala's southwestern port city of Muziris became a Spice Trade hub in about 3000 BCE.

The growth of trade is tightly linked to the history of India. Indian trade routes played a critical role as a connection between East and West, making it possible for large-scale and widespread trade to take place between civilizations. What began with the trade of obsidian in the earliest days of human settlement would grow into what we know as global trade today. And it was India that played an important role in pushing commerce, culture, and technology forward.

जानकी मन्दिर
नेपाल
२

Chapter 2

Foundations and Explorations

Indian history is complex. There are few time periods when most of the subcontinent was held by one power. The Greeks, Romans, and Persians dominated much of the ancient world, yet India was largely left alone. It was simply too difficult to bring large armies over the mountains on its northern border or across the sea to the south. As a result, smaller kingdoms were able to emerge and decline as the centuries passed. But trade was a large part of the subcontinent's large economy. Although kingdoms were independent, they universally welcomed traders and merchants from around the world.

The trade routes across the subcontinent and along the coasts developed over the course of centuries. Power shifts in the ancient world demanded new routes due to conflict, economic interests, and changing understandings of weather.

Opposite: *Indian kingdoms were among the first to use coinage, which revolutionized the way trade was conducted.*

This painting is called Vasco Da Gama Landing Near Calicut. *Da Gama was the first to reach India from Europe by sea. He opened up new routes for the spice trade.*

In this chapter, we will learn about the powers that controlled trade in India throughout its history, as well as some of the most famous routes that connected India to the world.

History of Indian Trade Powers

Indus Valley Civilization

The Indus Valley Civilization was the first permanent, urbanized region of India. It is sometimes called the Harappan Civilization, because the city of Harappa was the first to be excavated in modern times. It was centered around the fertile **Indus River** floodplain in modern-day India and southern Pakistan. The civilization stretched along the western coast of the subcontinent and into the mainland.

Archaeologists have found evidence of religious rituals dating back as far as 5500 BCE. They have also found evidence that more permanent settlements with farming began around 4000 BCE. Within one thousand years, the cities of the Indus Valley Civilization would rival those in the Mediterranean as modern urban centers of trade and commerce.

The cities of Mohenjo-daro and Harappa have shown historians how advanced the Indus Valley Civilization was and how important trade was to the economies of the cities that made up the empire. Mohenjo-daro and Harappa were established around 2500 BCE in modern Pakistan, far inland along the Indus River. Although we do not know how the Indus Valley Civilization was organized and ruled, both of these cities were well developed. They were two of the first major cities in human history, and homes

Harappa was one of the greatest cities of its time, and it was a center for commerce and trade in the Indus Valley.

with bathrooms and drainage systems have been found. Mohenjo-daro and Harappa helped establish the Indus Valley Civilization as a trading force in the ancient world.

Trade played a large role in Mohenjo-daro and Harappa. It influenced the growth of cities, the advancement of technology, and the significant wealth people in the region were able to amass. It is believed that the Indus Valley Civilization interacted with nearby civilizations as early as the Copper Age, or around 4300 BCE. Artistic goods have been found that resemble styles popular in northern Iran, which points to trade. Between 3200 BCE and 2600 BCE, Harappa and Mohenjo-daro started growing into large cities. This was the same time that trade by caravan became common in cultures in modern Iran and Central Asia. That trade gave rise to the cities themselves, shaping the way people engaged with the economy.

Trade allowed people in Mohenjo-daro and Harappa to develop specific sets of artisanal skills, including metalworking and pottery-making. People living in cities were often merchants, traders, and artisans. Hand-made goods included seals and tools made of bronze or copper, dyed clothing, and jewelry. Animals and surplus food were also traded.

Technology played a large role in helping the Indus Valley Civilization become traders and merchants. Standardized weights and measures were used throughout the area. Standardization made it possible to accurately and easily track goods and amounts that were being traded. There is early evidence of the use of wheeled carts and flat-bottomed boats, which would have made transporting large amounts of goods possible.

The Indus Valley Civilization was one of the first in India to have widespread trade relations, and their routes were among the earliest. Although we do not know the exact details of their trade relations, there is evidence that they traded by both land and sea with peoples in modern Afghanistan, Iran, Iraq, Crete, and Egypt, as well as the Persian Gulf.

The Indus Valley Civilization began going into decline around 1800 BCE. Historians attribute the decline to various causes, including climate change, a decline in trade with Mesopotamia and Egypt, and disease. Although the cause is not firmly known, by around 1700 BCE, cities were largely abandoned as people moved eastward. In Harappa, evidence of the area's culture after the fall of the Indus Valley Civilization suggests that trade had broken down by 1300 BCE, with items such as previously imported shells no longer found.

Vedic Civilization

Following the fall of the Indus Valley Civilization, a gathering of **Aryan** populations from the north brought the beginning of Vedic Civilization. This civilization takes its name from the legendary Hindu texts written during this period called the Vedas. During this time, trade expanded once again and strengthened industries from metalworking to agriculture. Vedic merchants began making wine, pottery, and tanned leather goods. They also worked with gold, tin, and silver.

Traders were ranked higher than artisans and laborers on the social hierarchy. Although Aryans were a dominant ethnic group during this time, the Panis and others became the most successful traders. These groups amassed great wealth and significantly impacted the way the economy was run. Tension between the two groups did lead to conflict, which resulted in a change in how trade was run that favored Aryan ideals.

Persian ruler Darius I invaded Vedic lands in northwest India around 510 BCE, bringing an end to Vedic culture's dominance. In its place rose kingdoms that warred with one another frequently until a few empires remained. By 322 BCE, most of the Indian subcontinent was controlled by the Maurya Empire. In turn, the Maurya Empire dissolved into regional powers around 230 BCE.

Chandragupta II, pictured here on a coin, was one of the most powerful emperors in the Gupta Empire.

Colonial India

Until around 1500 CE, India was controlled by regional powers that together held around one-fourth of the entire world's wealth. This wealth made it the largest economy in the world at that time. The most powerful kingdoms, including the Satvahana and Mahameghavahana, controlled key trade routes. This changed with the arrival of European powers in the last 1490s, including Christopher Columbus.

Regional states were weakened by war. Kingdoms were unable to fight against British, French, Dutch, and other European forces that sought to control the lucrative trade out of and through India, including the Spice Trade. European powers fought one another as they sought to control the industrious Indian subcontinent.

The British East India Company was established in 1600 to govern British trade rights in the East Indies, including commodities like salt, silk, indigo dye, and tea. Through the company, Britain was able to establish the earliest colonial control of India. Some, like the Mughal Emperor Shah Alam II, fought against growing British influence. Yet Great Britain was eventually able to secure control of vast areas of India, including all industry. Great Britain controlled most of India by around 1850, calling the subcontinent the "crown jewel" of the British Empire. Until independence in 1947, India's trade was controlled by foreign powers. Foreign control left the infrastructure and culture of trade greatly diminished for decades after power was returned to local rulers.

The Spice Trade

India traded in many goods and along many routes, but the Spice Trade is perhaps the most legendary in India's history. The Spice Trade was one of the earliest established trade networks in the ancient world, dating to around 3000 BCE. It was a key part of trade with Greece, Rome, and Asia. Widespread trade of spices allowed India to have cultural influence among cultures on the Indian Ocean. It also attracted European powers to the subcontinent in the fifteenth century, and it was a significant driver of the global economy for centuries.

The Indian Spice Trade was centered around Kerala, a coastal city in the southwest of India. Traders from Egypt and Arabia traded in spices with India along both land and sea routes. Routes connected India to Africa, China, and the Mediterranean. By 100 CE, the Spice routes stretched from New Guinea and Japan in the Pacific Ocean to Great Britain in the northern Atlantic, and as far south as Mozambique on the coast of Africa. Land routes spread from northern China through the Caucasus and into modern Turkey.

Spices were not the only goods traded via these routes. In fact, the sea routes were sometimes called the **Maritime** Silk Road. Food, jewelry, wood, metals, cloth, and other goods were also traded along the Spice Routes. Most importantly, information was also carried along these routes, spreading knowledge and news from around the world to ports of call.

But the spices themselves were in high demand, due in part to their scarcity in many parts of the world. Spices like cinnamon and pepper, which are not native to some parts of the northern hemisphere, revolutionized cooking. Spices were also used as perfumes, for dyeing cloth, and as incense. Spices were used as medicine and in rituals. In some cases, they became part of myths.

All of these uses, along with the rarity of some spices, made them extremely valuable. Control of the routes was held regionally, bringing great wealth to the empires or states that took a cut of the lucrative trade. India was able to position itself as the pathway between the East and West, making them a key part of the journey. Indian cities and exports appear in writing from Arabia, China, Greece, and Rome, all of which honor the part India played in keeping this massive network of trade routes and merchants flowing.

Land and Sea Routes

The Spice Routes were just a few of the routes that crossed the Indian subcontinent or stopped in its ports. Many more developed over the years and were used to transport many goods and cultural items. Some of these routes played important roles beyond trade, and some remain in use today.

The Grand Trunk Road

The oldest of these land routes was the Grand Trunk Road, which was in use during the third century BCE. It connects Bangladesh in the east to Kabul, Afghanistan in the west, making it one of the longest roads in Asia at about 1,600 miles (2,574.9 km). The road was a key trade route for its entire history, connecting the far eastern boundary of India with the Middle East. It has carried traders, migrants, armies, and visitors during its storied history. In his famous novel *Kim*, author Rudyard Kipling writes:

> Truly the Grand Trunk Road is a wonderful spectacle. It runs straight, bearing without crowding India's traffic for fifteen hundred miles—such a river of life as nowhere else exists in the world.

The Grand Trunk Road has undergone several periods of change since it began. Sher Shah Suri, leader of the northern Sur Empire, is among the most famous to have extended the road during his reign from 1486

CE to 1545 CE. Under Sher Shah, a culture of inns was established along the route that still stands today. He also planted trees to protect travelers and traders from the elements. During the colonial period, the British made improvements of their own to the road, which they used for military movements.

The Incense Routes

The Incense Routes were another trade network that remained important for generations. They were established around the seventh century BCE. The routes connected the Levant, Egypt, Arabia, and India by land. They were used to transport incenses like frankincense and myrrh, spices, stones, silk, wood, precious metals, and other luxury goods.

The Greeks attempted to find a way around land routes, which were controlled by kingdoms in the Levant and Egypt. However, they failed in circumventing them for many years. The Greeks only made direct contact with India when the merchant Hippalus discovered a passage through the Red Sea to the Indian Ocean in the first century BCE. This discovery changed the way the Greeks understood the geography of the world. And the passage allowed them to expand relations directly with the empires and kingdoms of India. The stage was set for the substantial Indian-Roman trade networks that would evolve during the early years of the **Common Era**.

Around that time, Ptolemaic Egypt (a Greek kingdom in Egypt) was used as a base for direct relations with India. Merchants traveled through the Red Sea and around Arabia to cross the Indian Ocean to get there. These sea routes weakened the monopoly Arabia had on trade. Before this time, the port of Aden was a main port used by ships crossing the Indian Ocean. Although it would remain part of the trade networks of the region, it was no longer as stable as it once was. Using the port of Myos Hormos on the Red Sea as a starting point, ships would venture to the Indus delta where once the Indus Valley Civilization had thrived. Roman historian Strabo wrote of the increase in trade: "I learned that as many as one hundred and twenty vessels were sailing from Myos Hormos to the subcontinent, whereas formerly, under the Ptolemies, only a very few ventured to undertake the voyage and to carry on traffic in Indian merchandise."

In the first years of the Common Era, Roman and Indian trade relations flourished as navigation abilities, understanding of seasonal winds, and a more complete grasp of the geography of coasts made it easier than ever to establish trade routes. The route from Rome to India crossed the Mediterranean, the modern Sinai Peninsula, along the coast of Arabia and along the entire coastline of India. From there, land routes connected Rome to China and sea routes continued down the coast of Africa.

After the Roman-Persian wars in the sixth century CE, Indian trade focused on Asia with limited trade with the Byzantine Empire in the north. When the Ottomans took control of the land routes between Asia and Europe, Europeans were essentially closed off. European powers then began their **Age of Discovery** in the fifteenth century CE. This time period was also the beginning of the Colonial period in India. And the Colonial period would affect Indian trade for decades.

Crossing the Indian Ocean

There were many discoveries that made trade with India easier for global powers. Perhaps the two most important were the full understanding of how the Indian Ocean was impacted by **monsoon winds** and what the region looked like. Until the nature of the Indian Ocean was understood, trade took place at the Arabian southern port of Aden. There, ships from Egypt, Greece, and India met to exchange goods. Geographers at the time believed that the Indian coast ran east to west rather than north to south. This shows how little was understood of that part of the world at the time!

That changed in around 118 BCE. Eudoxus of Cyzicus, possibly along with navigator Hippalus, was asked by Egyptian Pharaoh Ptolemy VIII to go with an Indian sailor who said he could take the two men to India directly. The journey was a success, and Eudoxus of Cyzicus made a second trip two years later. This was a journey that was rarely done because it was considered dangerous, and it often took an extremely long time as the ships had to stay close to the coast in order to stay on track. But Indian ships had been making the journey across to Arabia for centuries and knew the patterns of the monsoon winds that could drive a ship off course or bring it safely into port. By sharing that information with the Greeks, the Indian merchant had helped to open up direct trade between the two civilizations.

Chapter 3

Goods and Services

Indian trade has always been built on a wide range of goods and cultural exchanges. The subcontinent itself is rich in natural resources. These resources allow traders to export goods ranging from precious stones to spices to wood. Artisans also developed styles that were in demand across the ancient world and into modern times. Imported raw materials were processed by artisans into jewelry, art, or other goods that were in high demand elsewhere. Today, India still trades in some of the same commodities: precious stones, metals, and grains are a few examples. But **petroleum**, vehicles, and pharmaceuticals are also among their top exports, while electronics and oil are among their highest **import** commodities.

In this chapter, we will learn what goods India has traded over time, as well as some of the aspects of culture that they spread through trade relations.

Opposite: *The Grand Trunk Road, shown here between Kabul and Jalalabad, was one of the most important roads in history.*

The spice trade brought great wealth to India, but it also brought colonial powers eager to capitalize on its value.

Food and Animals

Food made up a significant portion of India's trade throughout history. The region's fertile flood plains provided farmers with a surplus of product that was traded for other goods. Clarified butter, pickled fruits and vegetables, honey, and wine were common exports, as well as grains and livestock.

Spices such as cloves or pepper were widely traded in both Asia and the Mediterranean, and eventually with Europe. These were used in cooking, to dye clothes, and as perfume or incense. Today the widespread use of pepper, cardamom, cinnamon, cloves, ginger, and other spices that originated or grew in India can be traced back to early influence as a result of trade. Spices were considered a luxury good for most of human history, rare and expensive enough that only elites had regular access to them. What's more, middlemen along the trade route would often create stories about how difficult the spices were to acquire so that they could justify higher prices. In one story from the fifth century BCE, the Greek historian Herodotus was told by a merchant that giant birds guarded the world's cinnamon supply and that men had to steal their nests in order to harvest the spice.

Tea, however, was not an original export of India. It was introduced by the British, who began large-scale production of tea varietals. Today, India is one of the world's leading exporters of tea, including the famous Assam, Ceylon, and Darjeeling varieties.

There is evidence that Indian animals were also traded with Rome, where exotic animals were prized as pets and for organized sport. Frescoes in Roman villas depict capturing animals native to India, including Indian elephants, Indian peafowl, and rhinoceros. Birds and monkeys were used to entertain guests. Lions, leopards, and other big cats were used in games. It is believed that animals were captured in India before being transported back to Roman territory via ship. Animal pelts and leather, particularly made from the skins of exotic animals, were also valuable trade commodities.

Goods

Many raw materials passed through India en route to other places in ancient times. Others were used by Indian artisans to make manufactured goods, such as jewelry. India is also rich in natural resources, making it an exporter itself.

Raw materials found in India were among the most valued of their time. Precious metals like gold, silver, lead, and bronze were valued for jewelry, artwork, and ritual decoration. Wood was also valued, due to the lack of naturally growing trees in parts of the Middle East and Mediterranean. India was also a route for other prized goods, including copper, wool, and incense. There also many precious stones traded through India, such as lapis lazuli, amethyst, jade, and mother of pearl. Some of these were traded as they were, but others were used to manufacture other goods before being traded.

Among the goods available from Indian ports were practical items, like needles for sewing, utensils for cooking, and buckles for clothing. Others were more stylized, such as ivory cylinders and metal pots. Terracotta was used to make toys, carts, and figurine animals. Beads were made with precious goods like gold, shell, and agate. Cloth printed with woodblocks, a system of creating repeated patterns with dye and wood-cut blocks, was also a popular item for export.

In an ancient text called the *Periplus*, the goods traded through the port city of Barigaza were listed as:

> Wine, Italian preferred, also Laodicean and Arabian; copper, tin, and lead; coral and topaz; thin clothing and inferior sorts of all

Dyeing fabric remains an important part of India's craft tradition. Cloth was one of India's main exports in ancient times.

> kinds; bright-colored girdles a cubit wide; storax, sweet clover, flint glass, realgar, antimony, gold and silver coin, on which there is a profit when exchanged for the money of the country; and ointment, but not very costly and not much. And for the King there are brought into those places very costly vessels of silver, singing boys, beautiful maidens for the harem, fine wines, thin clothing of the finest weaves, and the choicest ointments. There are exported from these places spikenard, costus, bdellium, ivory, agate and carnelian, lycium, cotton cloth of all kinds, silk cloth, mallow cloth, yarn, long pepper and such other things as are brought here from the various market-towns.

Cultural Exchange

Throughout history, one of the most important impacts trade has had on the civilizations that interact is the cultural exchange that takes place. These exchanges have changed religion, language, literature, architecture, music, and social symbols in ways that are both subtle and grand, but all are critical in the evolution of mankind.

As a meeting point between East and West, India played a unique role in the blending of numerous cultures. Cities emerged as cultural epicenters. Merchants and traders shared new techniques with artisans, exchanged news from around the world, and spread new ideas. Buddhism, Islam, and Christianity all came to India via trade, and found people open to different cultures and faiths. For much of history, trade routes were the primary way that information was shared across large distances, making them important for communication as well as the economy.

Indian influence can be seen in architecture, fashion, jewelry, and cuisine around the world. Equally so, the influence of those with whom they traded can be seen in India, such as **Hellenistic** architecture in the north or the widespread popularity of tea today. Indian culture also made its way to the Western world through the British and other European powers, influencing fashion and food. Patterns like calico and Iranian paisley became extremely popular in England from the 1700s. By removing the middlemen of North Africa and Arabia, the prices of spices went down considerably. This made them available to more of the population.

Exports Today

Colonialism in India greatly impacted Indian trade relations with the rest of the world. India gained independence from the British in 1947. At that point, the Indian government focused on a policy of **protectionism**. The government also intervened in business. Many industries were nationalized and regulations created a great deal of hassle for those hoping to do business in India.

This strangled trade. **Tariffs** around 200 percent made it difficult for countries to do business with India. Attempts were made to fix the economy in the 1960s and 1980s. Yet it wasn't until a near bankruptcy in 1991 almost threw the country into

The Silk Road

The Silk Road is one of the most legendary trade routes in history, connecting China and the South Pacific to the Mediterranean and Europe. The routes, which crossed land and sea, are associated with Chinese silk, a lucrative luxury good that has been prized for centuries. The Silk Road passed to the north of India, and the sea routes included stops at Indian ports. The Spice Routes were also associated with the Silk Road, sometimes being called the Maritime Silk Road.

The Silk Road is believed to have existed in some form as early as 1000 BCE, or possibly slightly earlier. Silk that could have been made in China was found in excavated Egyptian sites, but the material was also made in the Mediterranean and Middle East. When Alexander the Great spread the Greek Empire into Central Asia, he established what would become a significant stop on the Silk Road in 329 BCE. Under the Chinese Han Dynasty around 130 BCE, the Chinese empire began setting up relations with Central Asian civilizations, Greece, India, and the Middle East. The Silk Road remained in use until around 1720 CE.

Along the Silk Road, information and culture passed as well as goods. The Silk Road brought Buddhism and Islam into contact, and spread news to the farthest reaches of the ancient world. But it also brought danger; it is believed that the Black Death traveled along the Silk Road to Europe.

crisis that effective reforms were introduced. By cutting regulations, lowering tariffs and interest rates, and putting an end to public monopolies in key industries, India was once again able to become a leading trade country on the global market.

Today, India is the eighteenth largest export economy in the world, exporting around $310 billion worth of commodities and importing $447 billion worth of commodities in 2015. The country's greatest exports include refined petroleum, jewelry, rice, stone, artistic goods, and cars. Imports include gold, diamonds, cotton, and oil. Cultural exchanges are still an important part of trade with India as well. Bollywood, which refers to the Hindi film industry centered in Mumbai, is one of the largest in the world. Much has changed since the early days of international trade. However, India still maintains close trade relations with the states of what was Arabia and China, as well as Europe and the United States.

Chapter 4

The Major Players

Trade brought India into contact with all of the leading powers in history, from the Romans to the Chinese to the British. Although India was largely left alone by conquering powers, each change in power did impact trade, for better or worse. Change was nearly constant in and around India, yet trade remained largely stable throughout most of history. In this chapter, we will learn about the powers that shaped global trade and played a role in India's land and sea routes.

The Indian Empires

The Chera Dynasty

The Chera Dynasty was a long-lasting empire on the southwestern coast of the Indian subcontinent.

Opposite: *The Dashavatara Vishnu Temple is a Hindu temple established as early as 320 CE.*

It included Kerala, the city from which the Indian spice trade flourished for centuries. The kingdom was established around the third century BCE and lasted until around 1124 CE. This longevity is remarkable given that the Cheras were often at war with neighboring kingdoms.

Despite their frequent fighting with the nearby Pandyas and Cholas, trade was not interrupted. This trade allowed the coastal kingdom to become extremely wealthy. The Cheras established relations with Asia, Greece, Rome, and others along the Spice Routes. The area where their kingdom sat is rich in rivers connecting to the Arabian Sea and spices. Windy conditions made reaching their coast fairly easy. Along with spices, ports under Chera control traded in lucrative goods like ivory, pearls, and timber. They gathered Roman, Greek, and Mesopotamian gold in exchange for these and other commodities. But when Rome went into decline in the second century CE, the Cheras began losing power as trade lagged. They held on until the 1100s CE, eventually falling to conquering neighbors.

The Maurya Empire

As we learned previously, the Maurya Empire was one of the few to control vast areas of the Indian subcontinent and parts of neighboring modern countries, although only briefly. The Maurya Empire was founded in 322 BCE and held all but the far southern reaches of the subcontinent. It fell by 185 BCE and was replaced with smaller kingdoms.

Trade flourished under the Maurya, due in part to the stability of central control. The empire put in place standardized systems of finance and security, making it simple and safe to do business with them. **Jainism** and Buddhism both came to the empire through trade, bringing with them social reforms and ideologies that emphasized nonviolence. The empire was at peace for many years. This was a rarity on the subcontinent in antiquity and allowed the state to focus on expanding economic activities and solidifying industries like agriculture. They introduced a common currency, and the army moved quickly against bandits seeking to steal or do harm to merchants and traders. The trade relations the Maurya were able to establish were extensive and lucrative, making trade a key part of the economy across India.

The Satavahana Dynasty and Kushan Empire

The Maurya fell in 185 BCE and were replaced by smaller kingdoms. One of those was the Satavahana Dynasty, which controlled the eastern coast of the subcontinent. They maintained close trade relations with Rome and expanded maritime trade. They also developed trade relations with other kingdoms in India, such as those to the south.

In the early Common Era, the Kushan Empire emerged and controlled a great deal of the northern Indian subcontinent, as well as parts of modern Afghanistan and stretching eastward into China. The Kushan are notable for the adaptability to local religion and customs, willingly embracing **Zoroastrianism**, Buddhism, Greek worship, and Hinduism—depending on what territory they held.

Trade was important to the Kushan economy, and they connected maritime trade with the Silk Road by controlling parts of both. The empire had trade relations with China in the east and Rome in the west, and cultural exchanges were common. The Kushan were particularly helpful in spreading Buddhism along the Silk Road, and they exchanged artistic goods with the Romans frequently. The Kushan Empire fell into two halves around 225 CE, and the western empire was defeated by the Persians in 248 CE. The remaining Kushan held area was invaded and defeated, replaced by the Gupta Empire. The Gupta Empire, which lasted in the northeast from 320 CE to 550 CE, was a cultural center due to their advances in the arts and sciences and strong trade ties to the rest of the world.

The Vijayanagara Empire

In the early 1300s CE, the Vijayanagara Empire emerged in the far south of the subcontinent, uniting the area until 1646 CE. The Vijayanagara Empire was created in part to fight against Islamic forces invading from the north. The empire is referenced frequently in writings by European historians and travelers from the time period. Excavations have shown that they were exceedingly wealthy and powerful for most of their reign.

Trade was a key factor in their strong economy and brought new technology to the subcontinent. New techniques of irrigation enhanced the region's agricultural output. The empire also brought about new achievements in the arts, literature, and music. Strong central administration meant that the state received a cut of all trade done in the empire's three hundred ports. The empire's primary exports were spices, timber, precious stones, cloth, and crops. They also served as a point of contact between east and west, trading in metals, saffron, velvet, silk, and horses from around the world. During the reign of the Vijayanagara, the British and other European powers began making trips to India. By the time the empire fell from power, the European Age of Discovery had significantly hindered Indian control of trade.

Portuguese explorer Vasco da Gama revolutionized trade when he circumnavigated Africa to reach India.

The Persian Empire

The **Persian Empire**, centered in modern day Iran, was founded by Cyrus the Great in 550 BCE. It became one of the leading civilizations of the time. The empire would remain in existence, though with changing boundaries, until 1979. Then the short-lived Pahlavi Dynasty fell and the current Islamic Republic of Iran was established.

The earliest days of the empire were under the Achaemenid Dynasty. And even then, trade played an important role in the Persian economy. The first rulers established a tariff system that brought in the majority of the state's revenue. Expanded trade relations brought numerous commodities from the east and west into the empire. Trade with India was opened up after the empire established maritime bases along the Persian Gulf under Darius the Great around 500 BCE.

Trade was expanded further under the later Sasanian Dynasty, which ruled Persia from 224 CE to 651 CE. The Sasanians improved roads and bridges, maintained security on trade routes, and built more harbors to facilitate maritime trade. The Sasanians controlled parts of the Silk Road and another, smaller coastal route in the south. They also expanded relations with India, China, and into southern Russia.

The vast Safavid Dynasty began in 1501 CE and lasted until 1736 CE. The Safavids were the first to rule after the spread of Islam into Persia. The dynasty is widely considered the beginning of modern Persian or Iranian history. The Persian Empire grew very wealthy and powerful under the Safavids, due in large part to their role in trade. Their territory stretched

THE BOY CYRUS PLAYING THE KING.

Cyrus the Great, depicted here as a boy, would become one of the Persian Empire's most celebrated rulers.

from the Persian Gulf in the south to the border of Turkey in the north. It bordered the subcontinent on the east and the Islamic Empire in the west. Due to their position, it was nearly impossible to trade between the east and west via land without including Persia.

Maritime trade suffered under the Safavids due to the Portuguese efforts to cut out empires that imposed high taxes. Conflict between the Safavids and the Portuguese made the Persians rely on other European powers as allies. This gave the Persians an advantage when trade relations were established in the 1600s. But the sea routes were not as important to the Safavids as the Silk Road, which ran through a large part of their northern territory. Competition over commodities and routes put them in conflict with the Indians. Yet they maintained relations in order to maintain the trade routes that passed through both empires.

The Islamic Empire

The Islamic Empire became a major trading force following the rise of Islam in the Arabian Peninsula. Under the Islamic Caliphates, the Middle East and parts of North Africa were united. The empire controlled trade routes that passed from the east to the Mediterranean, along the Red Sea and coast of Arabia, and along the coast of North Africa.

Trade became an important source of revenue early on in the first Rashidun Caliphate, established in 632 CE. Caliph Umar imposed a tax on traders doing business in the Islamic Empire. However, this tax was only on goods that were sold rather than those brought into the empire for personal use. The Rashidun Caliphate saw a great increase in trade activities. Trade strength passed on when the Umayyad Caliphate came into power in 661 CE. The Umayyads introduced a vast bureaucratic system of administration. Their measures increased security and uniformity for business, industry, and trade.

The Abbasid Caliphate came to power in 750 CE, with territory spanning from Persia in the east into modern Turkey in the north and central north Africa in the west. Under the Abbasids, the Islamic Empire controlled most of the trade in the Indian Ocean. They also controlled the important Strait of Hormuz. The Abbasid Caliphate maintained a trade network in the Mediterranean and established trade relations directly with European powers. The Abbasids also controlled a stretch of the western Silk Road, which at that time remained a lucrative trade route. The Abbasids were a conquering power and through conquest spread Islam. But they also focused on opening trade relations with the areas in which they gained power. This ensured the continued revenue and stability that had made them powerful in the first place.

The Ottoman Empire was the final Islamic Caliphate, lasting from 1299 CE to 1922 CE. In 1922, it was divided between European powers following World War I. Centered in modern Turkey, the Ottomans controlled the coastal areas of North Africa, Egypt, the Levant, and the Middle East (except modern Saudi Arabia), as well as north into the Caucuses of eastern Europe. The Ottomans held a monopoly on trade between the East and West because they controlled portions of all land routes between the two regions. But Europeans used sea routes to get around the Ottoman tariffs, pushing the Ottomans towards stronger relations with the eastern powers, such as the Persians and the Chinese. The Ottomans made their major cities hubs of international trade, including Cairo in Egypt and Constantinople in Anatolia.

The Chinese Empires

China was the dominant trading force in the Far East. But much like India it was most often divided into various states and kingdoms. There is evidence that that the Shang Dynasty of 1600 to 1046 BCE established trade relations with regional kingdoms. Yet trade was undertaken most widely under the Han Dynasty of 202 BC to 220 CE. Under the Han, the Silk Road was formalized and used to establish trade relations with powers to the west. In the later years before the Common Era, the Han worked to establish diplomatic and trade relations with Southeast Asian powers, including those in India.

The Tang Dynasty of 618 CE to 907 CE expanded maritime trade. This brought great wealth to their empire. Under the Tang Dynasty, many foreign merchants came to live in China. Merchants brought with them vast cultural influences that shaped the port cities such as Guangzhou. Maritime trade was expanded again under the Song Dynasty of 960 CE to 1234 CE, when nomadic tribes cut the kingdom off from many land routes.

Trade continued to flourish until the 1500s, when the Ming Dynasty became increasingly isolationist. Europeans who reached China were sent away. Piracy became a much larger issue in the region as the state refused to engage in trade.

The Chinese kingdoms were powerful forces in trade, connected to India through various trade routes by land and sea.

The Portuguese Empire

The Portuguese became a trading force in the Indian Ocean during the European Age of Discovery. In 1488, explorer Bartolomeu Dias sailed around the southern tip of Africa, called the Cape of Good Hope. The new route allowed the Portuguese to forego routes through the Mediterranean, which at that time were controlled largely by the Ottomans.

In 1498, explorer Vasco da Gama made it to the coast of India. This opened a direct sea route for Europeans to take part in the spice trade. Prior to da Gama's journey, spices had been extremely expensive because they passed through many hands en route to Europe. Attempts to travel to the Indian Ocean via the south of Africa were universally failures and resulted in thousands of lives lost. When da Gama landed at Calicut on the coast of India, he ushered in a new era of trade in the Indian Ocean and of expansion of power for the European empires. A direct route revolutionized the trade in spices, silk, and other luxury commodities that passed through India.

The Portuguese were the sole European power in direct contact with India for several decades, making them immensely wealthy. That would change when France, England, and others began traveling via the same route that Dias had discovered around the south of Africa. In 1505, the Portuguese set up a formal colony in India. The colony would become one of the most powerful in the Portuguese Empire.

In recognition of his contributions, da Gama was named Viceroy of India in 1524. But Portuguese power in the region declined as other European powers began making the direct contact with India. Although the Portuguese maintained their colony in India until 1961, their influence was overshadowed by the British Empire's presence in the majority of the subcontinent.

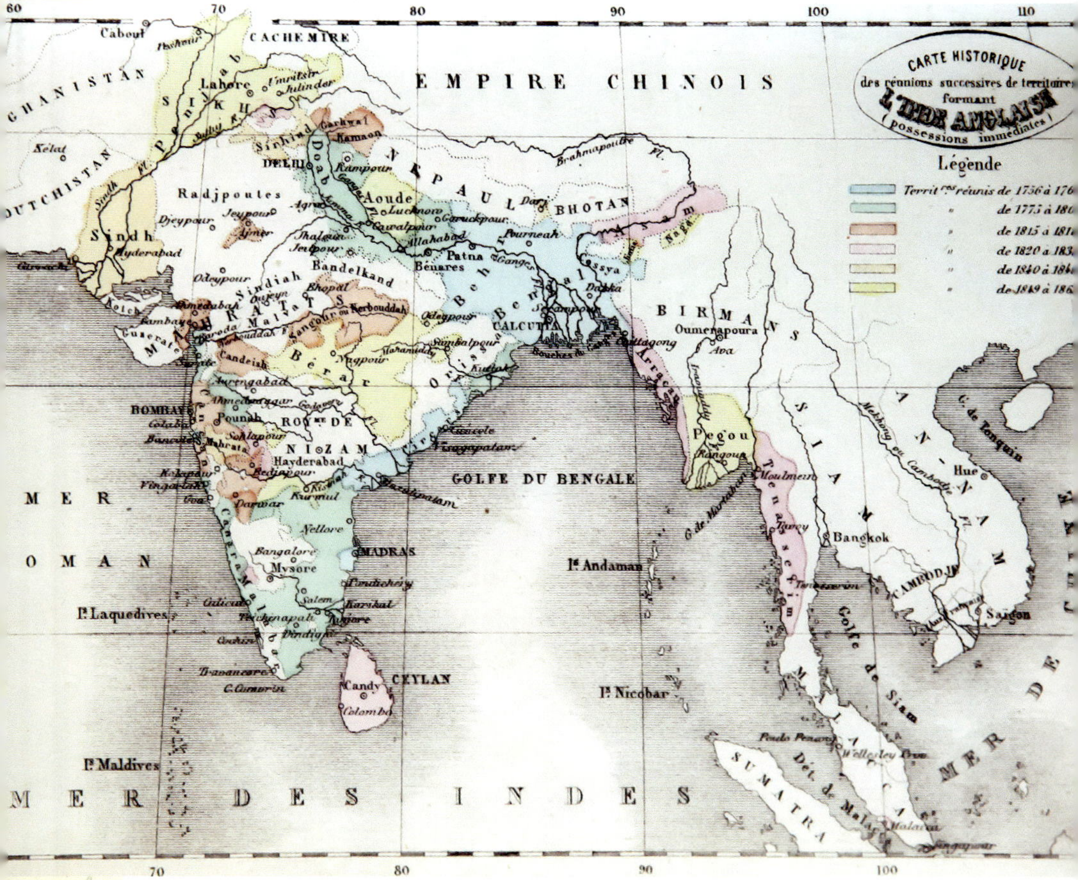

This map shows how British control of India evolved over time.

The British Empire

The British were present in India from around the early 1600s, when the British East India Company began exerting influence over trade and commerce in the subcontinent. Under the British East India Company, money gained from land revenue and industry deals made with the rulers of India helped finance further conquest of India. In turn, the British secured financial interests in other industries. By the mid-1700s, the British controlled much of the trade

Pliny the Elder

Trade has always played an important role in economic and cultural advances. But that doesn't mean that everyone has been in favor of increased trade relations. In fact, many states throughout history have adopted policies that isolate them from the rest of the world and cut off all or most trade. In the ancient world, one advocate for such a policy was Pliny the Elder, a Roman philosopher who did not see the benefit in spending Roman currency in empires around the world. In his final work, *Natural Histories*, Pliny wrote against the expensive trade with China, India, and Arabia, claiming that what Rome got in return was not worth the cost:

> We have come now to see journeys made to Seres [China] to obtain cloth, the abysses of the Red Sea explored for pearls, and the depths of the earth scoured for emeralds. They have even taken up the notion of piercing the ears as if it were too small a matter to wear those gems in necklaces and tiaras unless holes were also made in the body into which to insert them ... at the lowest computation, India and Seres and the [Arabian] Peninsula together drain our empire of one hundred million sesterces every year. That is the price that our luxuries and our womankind cost us.

out of India to Europe, making the British East India Company extremely profitable. Meanwhile, industry that had allowed India to thrive, such as the trade in indigo dye and salt, no longer benefited them at all.

It wasn't until 1858 that Great Britain formally established rule over India under the British Raj. Under the Raj, the sorts of practices established under the British East India Company were continued. British companies and individuals were given rights to industries in India. Many British interests exploited local labor for their own profit. Later, British policies gave rise to Indian Nationalism. The movement would eventually lead to the isolationist practices that hindered trade in the years after independence.

INDIA COM
REGIS & SENAT
1808

Chapter 5

The Effects of Indian Trade Routes

Given India's important role in global trade since the earliest days of civilization, their impact on culture is difficult to measure. Unlike the Phoenicians or the Greeks, India's role in shaping trade is ongoing and in many ways subtle. In ancient times, India was a meeting point between East and West. The region connected the greatest empires of the world to one another while passing along their own important contributions. The numerous trade routes that passed through India carried information, goods, new technology, religion, and other advances that pushed humanity forward.

In this chapter, we will learn about some of the ways Indian trade impacted the world around them and some of the ideas and technology that traveled via the routes that passed through the subcontinent.

Opposite: *The British East India Company solidified Britain's colonial rule over India. This coin features the company's emblem.*

The Spice Trade

The Spice Trade is one of the most famous in all of history, and for good reason. For thousands and thousands of years, the trade of spices through India, China, and Arabia shaped entire empires. The transmission of spices changed food preparation and served as the basis for entire myths. The hunt for spices led to the European Age of Expansion, the discovery of North America by Christopher Columbus, and eventually the colonization of India by the British.

Today getting spices is as easy as going to the local supermarket, but before the twentieth century, even spices like cinnamon were extremely difficult and expensive to acquire. Spices were as treasured as gold and, into the eighteenth century, spices from Asia were given as bonuses to workers. Spices were among the first goods traded on a global basis, making their way to the far reaches of the known world through sea and land voyages that could last months. We tend to think of global trade as something entirely new, made possible by easy communication and travel. However, spices were being used around the world before many well-known networks, like the Roman trade routes, were ever established.

Spices played many important roles in ancient and medieval society. They were used as perfume and incense, mixed together as medicine, and of course used in cooking. They were status items in Europe, a sign of wealth for the aristocracy that could afford them. People were paid in spices. Invading forces like the Visigoths in Europe demanded tribute not only in precious metals, but in pepper.

Spices like peppercorns and salt were prized items, and middlemen across the Middle East and Mediterranean knew that. This gave rise to myths about the origins of spices, including stories of daring required to get the spices from the few places they could grow. According to one story, pepper could only be found in India, where it was guarded by poisonous snakes. Of course, these myths were not true—spices grew widely in India and Asia, as well as Arabia and Africa. But it added to the allure of a good seen as luxurious and exotic, justifying ever higher prices.

Given the high demand throughout history, trading in spices was extremely lucrative. Empires throughout history sought to control all or part of the routes that carried spices across the world. With that control came immense wealth. Great kingdoms and empires were built in India, China, Persia, Rome, Arabia, and Egypt from trade profits. These sites gave rise to the most significant and prolific civilizations in history.

Spice even has links to the spread of Islam. The Prophet Muhammad, who introduced Islam to the Arab world, was a spice merchant. Without the spice trade, it is difficult to say if mankind would have advanced as they did during antiquity and the early Common Era.

Control of the Spice Trade was what pushed European powers to begin their greatest exploration efforts. The **circumnavigation** of Africa occurred in the 1400s, Christopher Columbus accidentally landed at North America in 1492, and Europe established colonies around the world. Although spices are less highly prized today, the markets in India where they originally held sway are still dominated by the industry. Kerala, where the Spice Trade originated in India, is still a huge player on the global spice markets.

Technology

Around the world, technology has always revolutionized the way we interact and trade. Early on in India's trading, the domestication of the camel and the development of wheeled carts made it possible for more cargo to be carried over longer distances. These developments seem simple to us today, yet in the earliest days of trading across civilizations, using camels and carts would have changed the lives of those who made their living on trade routes. Suddenly, more and heavier goods could make it across farther distances, opening the door to long distance trade of substantial means.

The maritime routes were also influenced early on by technology. Advances in ship building included the design of boats that rode higher in the water, featured weighted back ends, and protected cargo from rough waters. These features were crucial to making ships a sustainable means of transport for merchants. At the same time, the digging of canals and development of harbors created more stopping points for ships, bringing with them wealth and goods to areas that would have been passed over previously. Technology continued to shape trade throughout the centuries. As advances were made in navigation and shipbuilding methods, longer journeys with greater accuracy were possible. Indian ship building was considered a model for Europe as late as the 1700s, with French traveler Solvyns writing, "In ancient times the Hindus [Indians] excelled in the art of constructing vessels, and the present Hindus can in this respect still offer models for Europe."

Trade also shaped technology and the way language and the arts evolved. The use of paper became widespread through trade, as it was invented in China long before it came into use in Europe. Printing press technology also spread via trade routes, making access to education easier for people around the world. Alphabets and systems of measurement blended as they came into contact with one another. For example, the current numeral system used in the West originated in the Indian and Arab world. French scholar Pierre-Simon Laplace wrote:

> It is India that gave us the ingenious method of expressing all numbers by means of ten symbols, each symbol receiving a value of position as well as an absolute value; a profound and important idea which appears so simple to us now that we ignore its true merit. But its very simplicity and the great ease which it has lent to computations put our arithmetic in the first rank of useful inventions; and we shall appreciate the grandeur of the achievement the more when we remember that it escaped the genius of Archimedes and Apollonius, two of the greatest men produced by antiquity.

Trade also allowed cultures that were so far apart they never had direct contact to stay connected through intermediaries like India. China and Rome are an example of two great civilizations that did not interact directly with one another. They were still able to exchange goods and ideas through the long trade routes that connected them. Middlemen, like India, gained an understanding of both cultures. This was a vital asset that led to greater tolerance and diversity.

Buddhism started in India before spreading east. Today, statues and temples to Buddha are spread across the country.

The Spread of Religion

Among the many cultural exchanges made over the Indian trade routes, the spread of religion was one of the most influential. India is positioned at the epicenter of some of the world's most significant religious movements, including Hinduism, Christianity, Islam, and Buddhism. People of different faiths met and interacted along trade routes. Elements of these religions were shared with new populations around the world. The empires through which these merchants passed were often influenced by the new ideologies they brought with them.

Hinduism

Hinduism as we know it today emerged in India during the Vedic Period, between 500 BCE and 300 BCE. Although followers are not encouraged to convert others, Hinduism did begin spreading as trade relations with the rest of the world increased. By 200 BCE, traders and merchants were spreading Hinduism through Southeast Asia and possibly to Greeks. Hindu temples can be found in countries thought Southeast Asia today, including the famed temple at Angkor Wat. Hindu symbolism was adopted by royalty in places like Thailand and Indonesia. Today, these countries are not primarily Hindu. However, the influence of the spread of this particular religion can be seen in their respective cultures. A prime example is the adaptation of Vedic stories by people across the region.

Buddhism

Adoption of Buddhism was more widespread. The Buddha is said to have been born in northern India in the sixth century BCE. He was a member of an aristocratic family, but he turned instead to philosophy and developed a dogma based on his teachings. His followers were numerous, even including kings within the first centuries after his death. Monks spread Buddha's teachings throughout the Maurya Empire, which then included most of the Indian subcontinent.

Today we often associate Buddhism with China and the Far East. However, it was actually brought to China by Indian traders and Buddhist monks via the Silk Road. From around the first century CE, missionaries traveled with trade caravans into Central Asia. There they shared translated Buddhist writings and artworks. Merchants themselves were also apt to adopt the faith. By the fourth century CE, large parts of China had embraced Buddhism. Chinese pilgrims journeyed to India along the trade routes in order to visit the home of Buddhism.

By the ninth century CE, the spread of Buddhism began to decline. This was due to the rise of Islam in the Middle East. But by that time, Buddhism's place in Central Asia, China, and the island nations along China's border was firmly in place.

Islam

Islam, like Hinduism, does not emphasize conversion. But it spread along the Silk Road all the same. This was due in part to the many schools of thought that emerged from it in the years following the death of the Prophet Muhammad in 632 CE. Islam evolved as both a religion and a system of governance at the same time; therefore, it is unique among world religions. In the Quran, the Islamic holy book, there are guidelines for trade, taxes, and economic activity. These are still used or adapted by Muslim countries today. The Quran also supports good and honest trade relations. Caliphates paid particular attention to expanding trade with neighboring and conquered areas.

Sufism, a branch of Islam, is one example of how the religion spread. Sufi tradition appears across Asia through literature and the arts. Islam was a driving force behind scientific discovery, artistic expression, musical evolution, and the development of law and philosophy. Indonesia, which was introduced to Islam through the Silk Road, is the most populous Muslim country in the world today. India itself is home to the third largest Muslim population, with Pakistan, which became independent from India in 1947, in second.

Christianity

Early in the Common Area, Christianity also spread across Asia through trade routes. The dates when it is believed to have reached areas east of Jerusalem, where it was centered, show the slow and steady spread of the faith. It is believed to have reached India between the fourth and sixth centuries CE, traveling from India to China, Korea, Japan, and eventually Thailand in the fourteenth century CE. Just as Buddhist missionaries had used trade routes to spread their faith, Christian missionaries did the same for centuries, converting people across Asia to their religion.

While the spread of religion via trade routes was influential, it is also important to note that the interaction of people of different faiths was equally valuable. Trade routes presented a peaceful place for people of different backgrounds, cultures, languages, and beliefs to meet one another and share their thoughts. That diversity is remarkable, and undoubtedly led to the evolution of religion, thought, and ideas.

Cultural Exchange

Indian trade routes facilitated the exchange of architectural styles and fashion. Not only did India have significant influence on cultures with which they interacted, but those cultures also influenced India. The back and forth of ideas, styles, and techniques seen across the Silk Road, the Spice Routes, the Incense Routes, and other major trade networks that passed through India is a prime example of the importance trade has in culture.

Indian culture spread throughout history via trade routes. Buddhist imagery can be found throughout Asia, including in China, Java, and Japan. Indian influence can also be seen in Japan and China from the Gupta Empire. Another example is the Gandhara

The Taj Mahal is an example of how Indian architecture was influenced by neighboring civilizations and empires.

style. Gandhara is a school of northern Indian artistic expression influenced by Iranian and Syrian styles, making it a unique blend of regional powers.

Indian culture was also heavily influenced by Persia, due to interaction between rulers in northern India and Persian Muslim rulers in the Common Era. Persian language was once the official language of the Mughal Empire, only being abolished by the British in the mid-1800s. Persian influence can be seen in what we consider today to be iconic Indian architecture. The Taj Mahal, for example, combines elements of both Indian and Persian design.

India's influence can be seen very clearly in Europe. After the Age of Discovery, the subcontinent became an inspiration for everything from cooking to ship building to fashion. During the romantic movement of the late 1700s, Indian works like *Shakuntala* were translated into English and German for the first time.

That particular poem had a significant impact on literature, with poet Goethe writing:

> Wilt though the blossoms of the spring, the fruits of late autumn,
>
> Wilt thou what charms and enraptures,
>
> Wilt thou what satisfied and nourishes,
>
> Wilt though in one name conceive heaven and earth,
>
> I name, Skakoontala [Shakuntala], thee, and in that is everything said.

Another influential work translated in that time was *The Bhagavad-Gita* from the Vedic text *The Mahabharata*. Rooted in Hindu philosophy, the work influenced writers like Walt Whitman and Lord Alfred Tennyson.

In the 1800s, England saw a huge interest in Indian styles. This was driven in part by the Great Exhibition of 1851. The Indian Pavilion was one of the festival's most popular displays, featuring regional art and design. The pavilion inspired the widespread popularity of motifs and patterns traditionally used in Indian clothing and art, such as floral designs, paisley, and embroidery patterns. During her reign, Queen Victoria was particularly interested in Indian culture. She even learned a regional language called Hindustani and commissioned an Indian style hall for one of her residences.

But Indian styles adopted by the West weren't without controversial impact. Most often they were influenced by Orientalism, or a school of thought that saw the East as exotic and quaint. Orientalists thought the East was full of innocent but uncivilized peoples. Decorative goods like plates showed India as old-fashioned. This contributed to the public sense that India, and the rest of the East, needed to be modernized through colonization. In turn, British people began to support the expansion of the British Empire.

Americans were equally as taken with India, with Mark Twain describing India as:

> The land of dreams and romance, of fabulous wealth and fabulous poverty, of splendour and rags, of palaces and hovels, of famine and pestilence, of genii and giants and Aladdin lamps, of tigers and elephants, the cobra and the jungle, the country of hundred nations and a hundred tongues, of a thousand religions and two million gods, cradle of the human race, birthplace of human speech, mother of history, grandmother of legend, great-grandmother of traditions, whose yesterday's bear date with the modering antiquities for the rest of nations—the one sole country under the sun that is endowed with an imperishable interest for alien prince and alien peasant, for lettered and ignorant, wise and fool, rich and poor, bond and free, the one land that all men desire to see, and having seen once, by even a glimpse, would not give that glimpse for the shows of all the rest of the world combined.

Not all things that traveled from the East to the West were cultural or beneficial. The bubonic plague is believed to have traveled from China through India to Europe. Disease spread through trade fairly easily throughout history. Rats carrying infections boarded ships and carried illness to other parts of the world. The outbreak of the disease in the 1300s, called the Black Death, killed around one-third of the world population at that time. India was not impacted during the Black Death; however, another outbreak in the late 1800s, which originated in China, killed over twelve million people on the subcontinent.

Colonialism

India's important position in trade made it an attractive place for European powers to colonize. Therefore, multiple states tried to gain a significant foothold on the subcontinent. The Portuguese were the first, followed by The Netherlands, France, Denmark, and Great Britain. But it was the last country—Great Britain—that eventually controlled the vast majority of India and the trade in and out of the country.

Colonialism brought a great deal of change to India. Under the British Raj, the country was modernized, infrastructure was updated, and institutions were introduced that eventually made up the backbone of the modern state. But British rule also did significant damage, including causing starvation, massacring civilians, and exploiting workers. The British tightly controlled all lucrative industries, including salt and textiles. They gave little back to the Indian people who made them wealthy.

Winston Churchill was the celebrated prime minister who led Great Britain through World War II. He has become an icon of imperial Britain, particularly

Ashoka

In the later years before the Common Era, Buddhism became one of the greatest cultural exports India contributed to the world. That is thanks in part to Ashoka, a Mauryan emperor who ruled from 268 BCE to 232 BCE. Ashoka ruled an empire that stretched from the Hindu Kush mountains to the southern area of the subcontinent, controlling all but the southernmost part of India.

Ashoka was the first emperor to embrace Buddhism, reportedly after witnessing the large scale of death during his war with neighboring Kalinga in 261 BCE. In 258 BCE, Ashoka proclaimed his new faith to the public with his Kandahar Edict, which was written in Greek and Aramaic. It read in part, "King [Ashoka] made known Dharma to men; and from this moment he has made men more pious, and everything thrives throughout the whole world."

His relationship with Buddhism shaped the way he governed, rooted in strength as much as a personal connection with his subjects. He was a patron of Buddhism and made it the state religion. He funded temples and monasteries and advocated for the spread of Buddhism throughout the region. Although he did not embrace non-violence, he did contribute greatly to the spread of Buddhism both in India and across Asia. His contributions gave rise to the widespread practice of the faith in China and the Far East. Ashoka became the role model for leaders who followed, as well as Chinese leaders who sought to support Buddhism.

given his outspoken and controversial statements about India. He once said of India, "I hate Indians. They are a beastly people with a beastly religion." During the Second World War, Churchill's imperial policies led to a famine that killed around three million people in Bengal. In response, Churchill said it was the victims' fault for having too many children. He also spoke often in opposition to Mahatma Gandhi, who led nonviolent resistance to British rule. Churchill said, "Gandhi-ism and everything it stands for will have to be grappled with and crushed," among other statements.

The attitude shown by Churchill is in part what drove colonialism in India and around the world. The British saw themselves as a modernizing force saving barbaric populations from themselves. The truth was far more complex. On one hand, Britain did provide vast infrastructure that today remains in use or has been built upon. In some places, including India, the British colonial authority also provided a framework for central authority, bringing stability and unity to areas that had been divided among smaller kingdoms.

But the legacy of colonialism cannot be understood without taking into account the poverty, loss of life, and lasting sense of exploitation that shaped states as they became independent. In the case of India, this led to policies of isolationism and nationalism that damaged the economy significantly, as well as conflict with the partitioned states of Pakistan and Bangladesh.

Chapter 6

The Future of Indian Trade Routes

Many trade routes and trading powers have come and gone throughout history. The Phoenicians, the Mesopotamians, and the Ottomans were all significant trading powers who shaped the way countries interact. But these powers and the routes they used faded into history or were adapted over time. India is an exception to this pattern, however. Although not all the routes that once passed through India are still in widespread use, the country remains a trading power.

Today, India is still an important trade country, with ties to countries all around the world. The twentieth century was difficult for the Indian economy, though. It took multiple decades for the Indian government to overcome the hardships

Opposite: *Today, Indian cities like Mumbai are still on the cutting edge of global trade.*

imposed by colonialism and poor economic policy. But since the 1990s, India has become a leading member of the global economy—thanks in large part to trade. This is a natural continuation of their legacy, from their role in the earliest efforts at trade to their importance in the major routes of the medieval period. There are still obstacles that the Indian government is working to overcome. Yet many believe India will remain one of the key trading forces on the global market.

In this chapter, we will learn about how trade in India evolved during the second half of the twentieth century and where it might be heading. We will also look at a few of the key routes that passed through India to learn how they came to an end or how they have been adapted to the modern world.

The Silk Road

The Silk Road thrived until the fifteenth century CE, undergoing several phases of development and expansion during its long time in use. When the Mongol Empire fell in the east and the Byzantine Empire began to decline, the unity that had defined the Silk Road began to collapse. The Silk Road was no longer seen as a viable, strong entity, and it eventually fell out of use around 1450 CE. Although the trade in silk continued, Europeans sought sea routes to bypass the high tariffs imposed by the Ottomans and other powers along the land routes, giving rise to the European Age of Discovery.

Today, the Silk Road's Tian-shan corridor route in China is considered a historic landmark. Cities along the old route honor the route's legacy. It is considered a UNESCO World Heritage Site, and the organization notes that:

> The massive scale of the trading activities fostered large, prosperous and thriving towns and cities that also reflect the interface between settled and nomadic communities in a variety of ways: the mutual inter-dependence of nomads and farmers and different peoples such as between Turks and Sogdians in the Zhetysu region; the transformation of nomadic communities to settled communities in the Tian-shan mountains, resulting in highly distinctive construction and planning such as semi-underground buildings; and in the Hosi corridor the planned agricultural expansion of the 1,000 mile corridor after the first century BCE as an agricultural garrison and its transformation to settled agricultural communities ... The Tian-shan corridor is an extraordinary example in world history of how a dynamic channel linking civilizations and cultures across the Eurasian continent, realized the broadest and most long-lasting interchange among civilizations and cultures.

In 2013, President Xi Jinping of China announced his intent to start a New Silk Road connecting China to Europe, calling it "One Belt, One Road." The route was inaugurated in 2016 with a train journey between eastern China and Tehran, Iran. The plan is for cities along the route to be hubs for both land and sea routes.

The Incense Route

The Incense Route was another heavily used network, connecting the Mediterranean to the Horn of Africa and India. The routes were an extension of ancient trade routes used by the Egyptians and Mediterranean traders. Trade along them was the strongest between the seventh century BCE and the second century CE. The goods traded along the routes were primarily luxury goods, like precious stones, animal pelts, woods, and textiles.

The Incense Route fell into decline in the third century CE, when political unrest and economic crisis in Arabia disrupted trade. Over time, the routes once used for incense fell out of favor as powers found other routes around Arabia. Like the Silk Road, the Incense Route is today considered a World Heritage Site, particularly the portion that ran through Oman and the Desert Cities in the Negev in southern Israel. UNESCO notes:

> The Nabatean towns and their trade routes bear eloquent testimony to the economic, social and cultural importance of frankincense to the Hellenistic-Roman world. The routes also provided a means of passage not only for frankincense and other trade goods but also for people and ideas.
>
> The almost fossilized remains of towns, forts, caravanserais and sophisticated agricultural systems strung out along the Incense Route in the Negev desert, display an outstanding response to a hostile desert environment and one that flourished for five centuries.

The Spice Trade

The Spice Trade was once one of the most expansive and important trade networks in existence, driving the growth of empires and the exploration of the world. India was the heart of that trade, a supplier as well as a stopping point for traders from Arabia and east Asia. When spices ruled the world, it was India who truly held the throne.

But much has changed since the days when spices were more valued than gold. Today we can buy spices at the supermarket, including exotic curry blends and varieties of more common offerings. It may seem that the Spice Trade is long gone, but that's not quite true. Spices are still a frequently traded commodity. Many are still grown in the areas of the world that once dominated the spice routes, including Kerala on the southwest coast of India.

Today no single country or region controls the flow of spices to the rest of the world. Technology has made it possible for many once-rare spices to grow in parts of the world where they were previously nearly impossible to obtain. The spice trade today is dominated by producers and wholesalers, who import spices from around the world and work with retailers. Some companies are replacing the countries that once sought to have a significant stake in the spice trade. However, these major companies don't make up a monopoly that totally blocks out competition. There are efforts to ensure that some spices that are iconic or unique to one region, such as Kampot pepper, are grown exclusively in the areas to which they are native.

In short, the Spice Trade is still thriving, even if it looks very different than it once did.

Post-Independence

After gaining independence in 1947, India was faced with a number of obstacles to rebuilding their economy. The country was largely impoverished, with low literacy and poorly developed industrial infrastructure. Their years under British rule made the government protectionist and focused on a mixed policy of self-sufficiency and modernization designed to ensure India could thrive as a sovereign state.

Under the policies introduced in the 1950s, large industries were controlled by the government. Therefore, the government oversaw education, healthcare, media, and communication. The country also introduced a five-year plan to develop infrastructure, the agricultural sector, and other key areas. But the system was weighed down by regulation and bureaucracy. This made it difficult to see progress.

By the 1970s, the economy was not growing, and the country was struggling to keep up with other regional powers. Trade was difficult for outside actors. Around eighty agencies were involved in giving approval before a company could do business in India! State policy was based on the idea of import substitution, or a reliance on internal sources rather than trade to provide for all of India's needs. This created an environment that stifled international business. India was largely isolated from trade markets.

In 1991, India went into an economic crisis that nearly bankrupted the country. The country was able to secure funding through the International Monetary Fund in exchange for reforms to their economy, including the reduction of tariffs, the breaking up of state monopolies, and opening the country up to trade and investment. Over the next ten years, the country implemented new reforms that further opened the country up to foreign investment and trade. They also worked to increase literacy, food security, and quality of life for more citizens.

The result of these reforms was staggering. The country went from foreign investment of $132 million in 1991 to $5.3 billion in 1995. India quickly became a global hub of information technology services. India joined the World Trade Organization, a global trade governing body, in 1995. In 2003, President A. P. J. Abdul Kalam signaled that the Indian government would remain forward looking, saying, "We will be remembered only if we give to our younger generation a prosperous and safe India, resulting out of economic prosperity coupled with civilizational heritage."

Indian Trade Today

Today, India is once again a global trading power. The nation has trade agreements with countries around the world. Indian leadership has strongly advocated for increased global trade. But the country struggles with a trade deficit, meaning they import more than they export. Imports for 2015 stood at around $447 billion worth of commodities, while exports were around $310 billion worth of commodities. This difference is significant; it means that India spends more on imports than it makes on exports, resulting in a net trade loss for the country.

India's primary exports are in some cases similar to those that made the country a trading power in the ancient world. Jewelry, metals, and grains

Jewelry, spices, and other goods have been important trade commodities for centuries.

are still among the top exports, along with refined petroleum, cars, and machinery parts. India is also a global power in information technology, an emerging market that makes them extremely competitive in the international economy.

There are still challenges facing India, including a high rate of poverty. But experts are optimistic that trade will remain steady in coming years. Some key areas that international trade regulators and observers have identified as continuing issues are remaining barriers to international investment, the country's trade deficit, and a tax code that needs to be updated along with labor laws. Any of these could once again cause the country's economy to stagnate and make trade less desirable for outside powers, although

Indian Prime Minister Narendra Modi has made trade a focus of his economic policy.

forecasts suggest that trade will continue growing in coming years.

Prime Minister Narendra Modi revealed in 2015 that his government plans to increase exports significantly, with hopes to top $900 billion by 2020. The country also hopes that Indian exports will become 3.5 percent of all global exports by the same year. His government will also establish new trade councils to help improve trade policy and implement obligations from the international community. All of these policies, along with new incentives for exports, are aimed at helping make up the deficit the country currently runs and make sure that Indian markets stay competitive.

Trade today looks very different from trade even one hundred years ago, but at its core it remains

In 2015, Modi traveled to the UK to discuss trade with David Cameron, then prime minister of Britain.

largely the same. Trade relations make up the backbone of international relations and cultural exchange, just as they did in antiquity. While the jargon and methods of trade are more high-tech than they once were, the way trade connects our world is still fascinating and important.

India has a long legacy of being part of that connection. From their role in the ancient world as a bridge between East and West to their importance as a stopping point for numerous important routes that shaped mankind, India has always been the heart of global trade. It was through India that spices, silks, gold, and religions passed around the world, building cultures and influencing the evolution of human history.

That is no less true today than it was centuries ago. The story of Indian trade is largely the story of human history. It shows the remarkable evolution that trade has undergone since the earliest days of human civilization. As Virchand Gandhi said in 1899, "In international commerce, India is an ancient country." Thousands of years after they first began trading with regional powers, India remains a global trading power, and will for many generations to come.

P. V. Narasimha Rao

P. V. Narasimha Rao was the ninth Prime Minister of India, serving from 1991 to 1996. Rao came to office just as one of the worst financial crises to hit India began, threatening the country with bankruptcy. It was under Rao that India began the economic reforms that completely revitalized their economy and re-established the country as a trading

As prime minister, P.V. Narasimha Rao helped save the economy from collapse and set it on a path toward prosperity.

power. Along with Financial Minister Manmohan Singh, Rao broke with long standing economic policies in order to save the country. This was a leap of faith that could have been a disaster. But it paid off, and today India is one of the largest economies in the world. Because of this, Rao is often called the "Father of Indian Economic Reforms."

But during his time in office, Rao gave Singh, a trained economist, most of the credit for the reforms. It was only after his death that people came to realize the remarkable role he played in mandating reform and encouraging changes to a system that was hindering India's growth. Later, an aide close to Rao named Jairam Ramesh said, "One thing is certainly true: the manner in which Rao handled the politics of the economic reforms was quite remarkable. He listened to everybody, and then did precisely what he wanted." His tight focus on ensuring the economic safety of the country has made him a nationally recognized hero. Rao passed away in 2004, living long enough to see his country emerge as a force in the global economy.

Glossary

Age of Discovery A period of exploration carried out by European powers from the fifteenth century to the eighteenth century.

Arabia A term referring to the Arabian Peninsula, made up of modern countries Saudi Arabia, Yemen, Oman, the Gulf Emirates, and others.

Aryan An ancient ethnic group that once lived in southern Iran and northern India.

British East India Company A private company established to manage British trade in the East Indies. It eventually gained control over most of India's trade, serving as a precursor to British colonial rule.

circumnavigation To travel around an entire landmass, such as an island or continent.

Common Era The current calendar used in the West. Also called the "Current Era."

exports Goods sold by a country to other countries.

Far East A term used to encompass East Asia, including Eastern Russia, Eastern China, and countries like Korea and Japan.

Grand Trunk Road An ancient road that connected the borders of modern India.

Hellenistic Related to Greek culture or history.

Horn of Africa The easternmost part of the African continent, made up of modern countries Djibouti, Eritrea, Ethiopia, and Somalia. It is believed to be where the ancient trading power Punt was located.

imports Goods bought by a country from other countries.

Incense Route A trade network that connected the Middle East and India to Europe.

Indus River A river that starts in Tibet and runs south through Pakistan and northern India to the Arabian Sea. The floodplain is very fertile, giving rise to the region's early civilizations and cities.

Indus Valley Civilization One of the first civilizations on Earth, based around the Indus River in northern India.

Jainism An early Indian religion with no central deity that was worshipped.

Levant A term used to encompass modern day Israel, Jordan, Lebanon, Palestine, Cyprus, and other Mediterranean-bordering states in the Middle East.

Maratha Empire One of India's great empires that controlled much of the area that makes up the modern country. It lasted from 1674 to 1818, ending as colonialism swept the region.

maritime A term that refers to things having to do with the sea, particularly commerce.

monsoon winds Seasonal changes in wind direction that affect sailing. In the summer winds blow southeast, while in the winter they blow northeast.

obsidian A natural glass created when lava cools rapidly. It was one of the first commodities traded widely.

Persian Empire Persia is located in what is today called Iran. The country was known as Persia until 1935, when the government requested that the international community use the domestic name Iran.

Phoenicians People of the ancient civilization of Phoenicia, located on the Mediterranean. Phoenicians dominated trade networks from 3000 BCE to around 1500 BCE.

protectionism An economic policy that aims to protect domestic industries by raising taxes on imports.

self-sufficient Describing policies that emphasize producing everything domestically and providing for all citizens' needs internally rather than relying on outside powers.

Spice Trade A global trade network and market in rare spices from Asia, the Middle East and Africa. It inspired the Age of Discovery.

subcontinent A term used to describe a large landmass that is attached to a larger continent but is easily distinguished from that whole. North America and India are both examples.

tariffs Taxes on imports or exports imposed by the state as a means to gather revenue.

Zoroastrianism An ancient monotheistic religion that emerged in Persia during the Bronze Age.

Bibliography

Bumbacher, Stephen Peter and Ann Heirman. *The Spread of Buddhism*. Leiden, Germany: Brill, 2007.

Chandra, Moti. *Trade and Trade Routes in Ancient India*. New Delhi, India: Shakti Malik, 1977.

Chaudhuri, K. N. *Trade and Civilisation in the Indian Ocean*. Cambridge, UK: Cambridge University Press, 1985.

Corn, Charles. *Scents of Eden: A History of the Spice Trade*. Tokyo: Kodansha International, 1999.

Gates, Charles. *Ancient Cities*. New York: Routledge, 2003.

Goldberg, Jessica L. *Trade and Institutions in the Medieval Mediterranean*. Cambridge, UK: Cambridge University Press, 2012.

Groom, N. St. J. *Frankincense and Myrrh: A Study of the Arabian Incense Trade*. New York: Longman, 1981.

Hansen, Valerie. *The Silk Road*. Oxford, UK: Oxford University Press, 2012.

Harland, Philip A. *Travel and Religion in Antiquity*. Ontario, CA: Wilfrid Laurier University Press, 2011.

James, Lawrence. *Raj: The Making and Unmaking of British India*. New York: St. Martin's Griffin, 2000.

Keay, John. *The Spice Route: A History*. Berkeley: University of California Press, 2005.

Krondl, Michael. *The Taste of Conquest: The Rise and Fall of the Three Great Cities of Spice.* New York: Ballatine Books, 2008.

Liu, Xinru. *The Silk Road in World History.* Oxford, UK: Oxford University Press, 2010.

Meredith, Robyn. *The Elephant and the Dragon.* New York: W. W. Norton, 2007.

Nabhan, Gary Paul. *Cumin, Camels, and Caravans: A Spice Odyssey.* Berkeley: University of California Press, 2014.

Pliny the Elder. *Natural History.* Cambridge, MA: Harvard University Press, 1992.

Possehl, Gregory L. *The Indus Civilization: A Contemporary Perspective.* New York: Altamira, 2002.

Prasad, Prakash Charan. *Foreign Trade and Commerce in Ancient India.* New Delhi, India: Abhinav Publications, 1977.

Tracy, James D. *The Rise of Merchant Empires: Long Distance Trade in the Early Modern World.* Cambridge, UK: Cambridge University Press, 1990.

Wild, Antony. *The East India Company: Trade and Conquest from 1600.* New York: HarperCollins, 2000.

Further Information

Websites

Ancient History Encyclopedia
http://www.ancient.eu
This online encyclopedia contains information on a range of historical civilizations and relations, including India's trade routes.

Asia Society
http://www.asiasociety.org
The Asia Society, a nonprofit think tank, presents historical information about various Asian issues, including trade across Asia.

The British Museum
http:///www.ancientindia.co.uk
The British Museum maintains a digital archive of information and artifacts from throughout India's history.

UNESCO World Heritage
http://www.whc.unesco.org
The website for this United Nations organization features information about the history, current status, and preservation of sites like the Silk Road.

Books

Bailey, Katharine. *Vasco Da Gama: Quest for the Spice Trade*. New York: Crabtree Publishing, 2007.

Frankopan, Peter. *The Silk Roads: A New History of the World*. New York: Knopf Doubleday, 2016.

Koestler-Grack, Rachel A. *Vasco da Gama and the Sea Route to India*. Philadelphia: Chelsea House, 1973.

Wood, Frances. *The Silk Road: Two Thousand Years in the Heart of Asia*. Berkeley: University of California Press, 2002.

Videos

"Crash Course World History #2: Indus Valley Civilization"
http://www.youtube.com/watch?v=n7ndRwqJYDM
Follow along as this short video outlines the importance of the Indus Valley Civilization.

"Crash Course World History #6: Buddha and Ashoka"
http://www.youtube.com/watch?v=8Nn5uqE3C9w
Learn more about the major figures of Buddhism.

Index

Page numbers in **boldface** are illustrations. Entries in **boldface** are glossary terms.

About the Author

Bridey Heing is a writer and book critic based in Washington, DC. She holds degrees in political science and international affairs from DePaul University and Washington University in Saint Louis. Her areas of focus are comparative politics and Iranian politics. Her master's thesis explores the evolution of populist politics and democracy in Iran since 1900. She has written about Iranian affairs, women's rights, and art and politics for publications like the *Economist*, *Hyperallergic*, and the *Establishment*. She also writes about literature and film. She enjoys traveling, reading, and exploring Washington's many museums.